Starting Preschool

This book belongs to

Place your star sticker here when you complete a page. See how far you've come!

Author: Carole Asquith

How to use this book

- Find a quiet, comfortable place to work, away from distractions.
- This book has been written in a logical order, so start at the first page and work your way through.
- Help with reading the instructions where necessary and ensure that your child understands what to do.
- This book is designed to help your child become better prepared for preschool. It focuses on the areas of learning within the Early Years Foundation Stage (EYFS), as used in preschools.
- If an activity is too difficult for your child then do more of our suggested practical activities (see Activity note) and return to the page when you know that they're likely to achieve it.
- Always end each activity before your child gets tired so that they will be eager to return next time.
- Help and encourage your child to check their own work as they complete each activity.
- Let your child return to their favourite pages once they have been completed. Talk about the activities they enjoyed and what they have learnt.

Special features of this book:

- **Stickers:** to be used in activities where instructed. The stickers are labelled with the page number, indicating where they are to be placed.
- **Progress chart:** when your child has completed a page, ask them to stick the relevant star on the first page of the book. This will enable you to keep track of progress through the activities and help to motivate your child.
- **Activity note:** situated at the bottom of every left-hand page, this suggests further activities and encourages discussion about what your child has learnt.
- **Certificate:** the certificate on page 24 should be used to reward your child for their effort and achievement. Remember to give lots of praise and encouragement, regardless of how they do.

Published by Collins
An imprint of HarperCollins*Publishers*
1 London Bridge Street
London SE1 9GF

HarperCollins*Publishers*
Macken House, 39/40 Mayor Street Upper,
Dublin 1, D01 C9W8, Ireland

© HarperCollins*Publishers* Ltd 2026

10 9 8 7 6 5 4 3 2 1

ISBN 978-0-00-877534-6

First published 2026

The author asserts the moral right to be identified as the author of this work.

All rights reserved. No part of this publication may be reproduced, stored in a retrieval system, or transmitted, in any form or by any means, electronic, mechanical, photocopying, recording or otherwise, without the prior permission of Collins.

Without limiting the exclusive rights of any author, contributor or the publisher of this publication, any unauthorised use of this publication to train generative artificial intelligence (AI) technologies is expressly prohibited. HarperCollins also exercise their rights under Article 4(3) of the Digital Single Market Directive 2019/790 and expressly reserve this publication from the text and data mining exception.

British Library Cataloguing in Publication Data

A Catalogue record for this publication is available from the British Library.

Author: Carole Asquith
Publisher: Fiona McGlade
Project editor: Chantal Addy
Design and layout: Sarah Duxbury
Cover design: Sarah Duxbury and Amparo Barrera
All images ©Shutterstock.com and ©HarperCollins*Publishers*
Production: Bethany Brohm
Printed in India by Multivista Global Pvt. Ltd.

Contents

How to use this book	2
I can draw my family	4
I know where I live	5
I know my numbers	6
I know some letters	8
I know more letters	10
I know my shapes	12
I know my colours	13
I know my animals	14
I can choose healthy foods	16
I know the days of the week	18
I know what I look like	19
I can wash my hands	20
I can brush my teeth	21
I can dress myself	22
I know the times of my day	23
Certificate	24

I can draw my family

- Draw a picture of your family at the beach. Don't forget to include yourself and any pets you may have! Find and use the beach stickers to complete the picture.

Talk to your child about the members of your family. If they have siblings, discuss who is older/younger and taller/shorter. Explain the names of the relationships between your family members such as brothers and sisters, aunties and uncles, grandmas and grandads.

I know where I live

- Sometimes fish live in a tank. Find and use the stickers to complete the picture of their home.

- Draw a picture of where you live. Remember to put a roof on and some windows and doors. Can you write the number on your door?

Well done! Add your star stickers to page 1.

I know my numbers

- Look at the number in the box. Put a circle around the same number in the row.

2	1	2	3	4	5
4	1	2	3	4	5
3	5	4	3	2	1
1	5	4	3	2	1
5	1	2	3	4	5

- This little rabbit has found some vegetables to eat. Place your stickers, then count the vegetables.

Put plastic or foam number shapes into a bag and ask your child to select one. Can they say the number? You could use them to count numbers 1 to 5 and then increase to 10.

- Use your stickers to find the animals at the zoo.

- Count the number of animals and circle below.

6   7   8   9   10

Well done! Add your star stickers to page 1.

I know some letters

- Start at the red dot and trace each letter with your finger. Place the missing picture sticker that starts with the same sound.

Help your child to start learning the letters in their name to prepare them for name recognition when starting preschool. Add more letters of the alphabet as they build their confidence. Remember to give lots of encouragement as you go!

- Place your letter sticker next to the picture that starts with the same sound.

Well done! Add your star stickers to page 1.

I know more letters

- Place the missing picture stickers, then draw a line to match each letter to the picture that starts with the same sound.

Use songs and actions to help your child remember the individual sounds to form a basis for phonic blending as they start school. It is important to learn the letter sound as well as the name of the letter to develop sound-blending skills.

y q

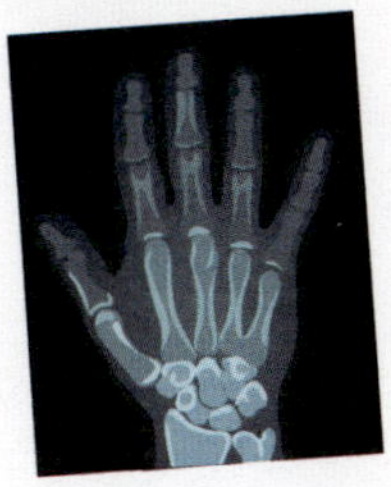

z

w v

x j

Well done! Add your star stickers to page 1.

I know my shapes

- Place the missing shape stickers, then draw a line to match each shape to the correct picture.

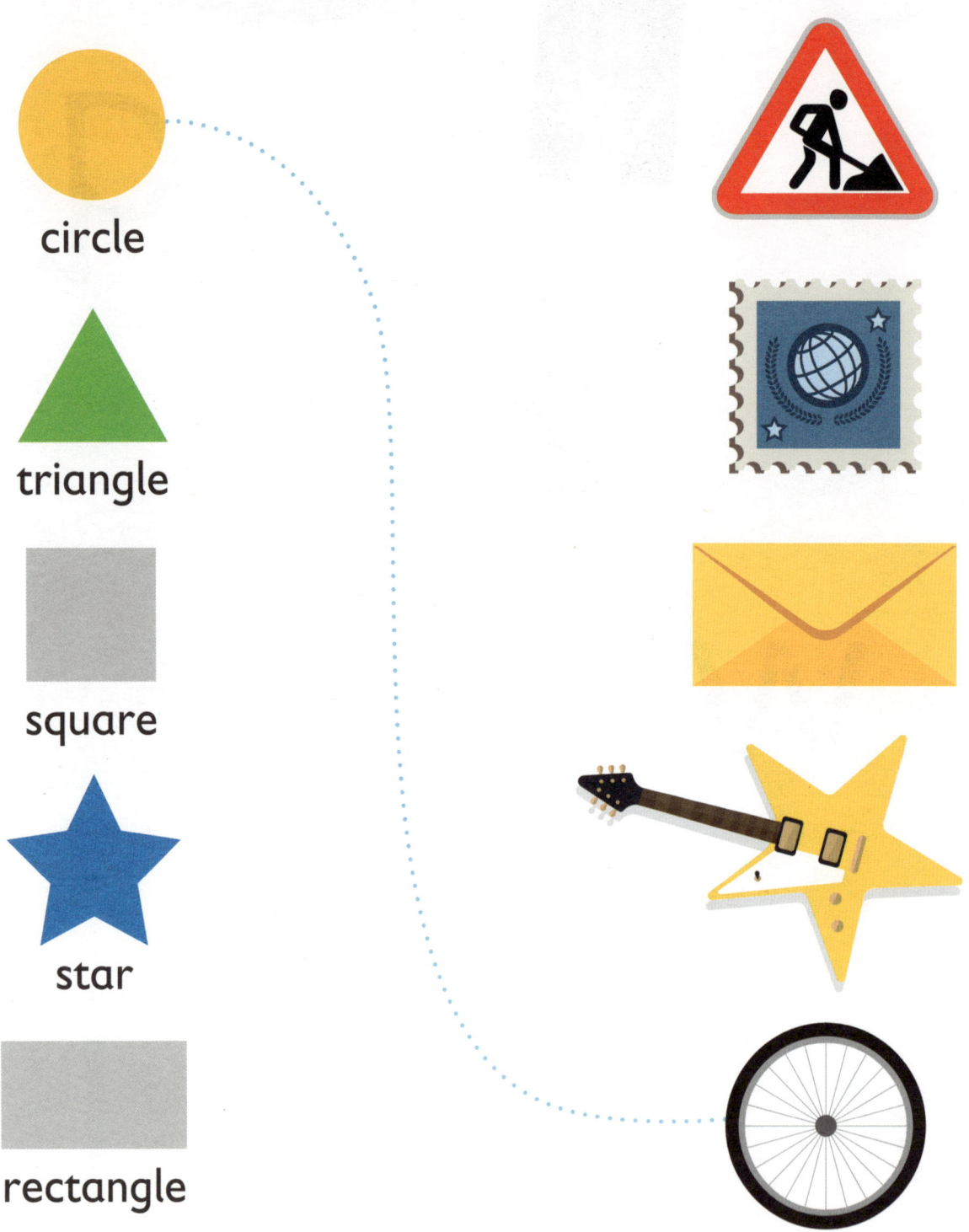

I know my colours

- Place the missing colour stickers, then draw a line to match each colour to the correct picture of the same colour.

Well done! Add your star stickers to page 1.

I know my animals

- Place the flamingo sticker and follow its footprints to find some friends. Name each animal and say what colour it is.

Choose books with real-life photographs of animals in it. Point to the animals saying the name and the sound it makes.

- Place the missing animal stickers, then draw a line to match each animal to its home.

Well done! Add your star stickers to page 1.

I can choose healthy foods

- Use your face stickers to show which foods are healthy or unhealthy.

Encourage your child to make healthy choices for meals. Providing healthy food from an early age helps them to develop a healthy balanced diet which should last throughout their adulthood.

● Add your food stickers to the correct lunchbox.

Healthy

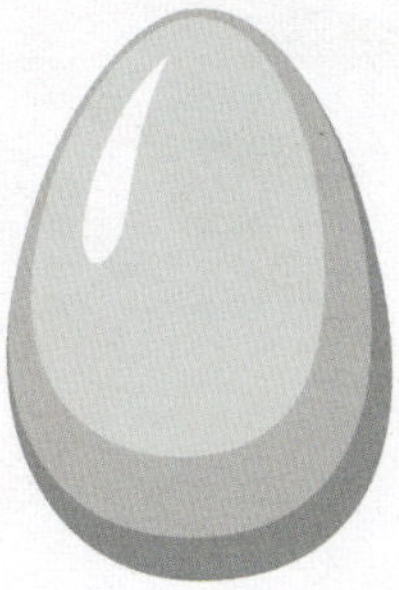

Unhealthy

Well done! Add your star stickers to page 1.

I know the days of the week

- There are 7 days in a week. Use your stickers to arrange the missing days in the correct order.

Sing a 'Days of the week' song with your child to help them learn the order of days in the week. Discuss with them their daily routine, highlighting activities to help them remember the order of the days.

I know what I look like

- Do you know what you look like? Draw a picture of your face using the outline as a guide. Remember your eyes, ears, mouth and eyebrows! Complete your picture by adding some hair.

Well done! Add your star stickers to page 1.

I can wash my hands

- You should always wash your hands after using the bathroom, before eating food and before helping in the kitchen! Use your number stickers to show the order for washing your hands.

Dry on a towel

Put soap on

Wet your hands

Rub together, don't forget the back!

Rinse them under the water

Adopting routines for hygiene is an important part of keeping healthy. Encourage your child to follow the procedures for hand washing after using the bathroom, before eating food and before helping in the kitchen. Use a tick chart for them to show when they have washed their hands. Make it fun!

I can brush my teeth

- Use your number stickers to show the order for brushing your teeth.

Spit out the toothpaste

Add toothpaste to your brush

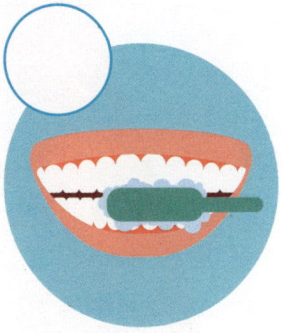

Rinse your toothbrush clean

Brush all of your teeth

- Use your face stickers to show which food and drink items are good or bad for your teeth.

Well done! Add your star stickers to page 1.

I can dress myself

- Can you dress yourself? Add the button stickers to the coat.

- Now practise fastening some buttons on your own coat.

Try to encourage your child's independence skills when caring for themselves. Start by putting on coats and then let them dress themselves. Practise buttons and zips on clothing whilst not wearing them until they develop their fine motor skills.

I know the times of my day

- Place the stickers to complete your daily routine.

At 7 o'clock, I get up.

At 8 o'clock, I eat breakfast.

At 10 o'clock, I play with toys.

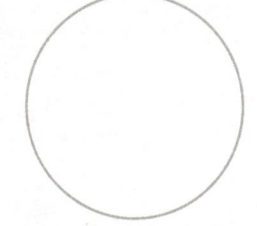

At 12 o'clock, I eat lunch.

At 7 o'clock, I go to bed.

At 5 o'clock, I eat dinner.

At 2 o'clock, I play outside.

Well done! Add your star stickers to page 1.